I didn't know that

you

can

jump

higher

on the

Moon

© Aladdin Books Ltd 1997

Produced by

Aladdin Books Ltd

28 Percy Street

London W1P 0LD

First published in the United States in 1997 by

Copper Beech Books,

an imprint of

The Millbrook Press

2 Old New Milford Road

Brookfield, Connecticut 06804

Concept, editorial, and design by

David West Children's Books

Designer: Robert Perry

Illustrators: Francis Phillipps, Ian Thompson, Rob Shone, Jo Moore

Printed in Belgium

Library of Congress Cataloging-in-Publication Data

Petty, Kate.
You can jump higher on the moon and other amazing facts about space
exploration / by Kate Petty ; illustrated by Francis Phillipps and Ian Thompson.
p. cm. — (I didn't know that—)
Includes index.
Summary: Focuses on our exploration of space by citing notable facts
discovered while visiting and investigating the moon and planets.
ISBN 0-7613-0564-5 (lib. bdg.). — ISBN 0-7613-0592-0 (trade hc)
1. Astronautics—Miscellanea—Juvenile literature. 2. Outer space–
–Exploration—Miscellanea—Juvenile literature. [1. Astronautics—Miscellanea.
2. Outer space—Exploration—Miscellanea.] I. Phillipps, Francis, ill.
II. Thompson, Ian, 1964- ill. III. Title. IV. Series.
TL793.P463 1997   96-43330
629.4—dc20   CIP AC

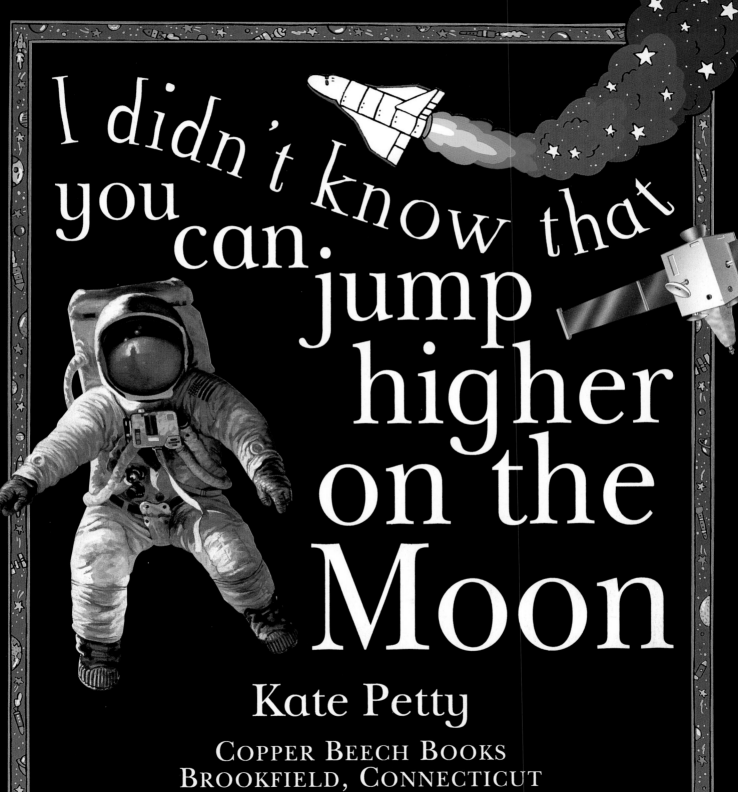

I didn't know that you can jump higher on the Moon

Kate Petty

COPPER BEECH BOOKS
BROOKFIELD, CONNECTICUT

I didn't know that

Introduction

Did *you* know that one day people will go to Mars? ... that trips to space will be possible for everybody? ... that aliens might really exist?

Discover for yourself amazing facts about space exploration, from the earliest attempts to today's regular trips by the Space Shuttle.

Look out for this symbol, which means there is a fun project for you to try.

Is it true or is it false? Watch for this symbol and try to answer the question before reading on for the answer.

! Don't forget to check the borders for extra amazing facts.

6

I didn't know that

rockets can travel at 25,000 mph. This is the speed needed to escape Earth's *gravity* and enter space. A steady 18,000 mph keeps the rocket in *orbit*. Modern rockets are used for launching *space probes* and *satellites.*

Satellite

Third stage

Second stage

First stage

Solid-fuel boosters

The rocket is pushed into space by three stages that burn up and fall away one by one.

Werner von Braun was the German inventor of the deadly V-2 rocket. Late he became the chief designe of space rockets in the U.S.

The Chinese invented rockets nearly 1,000 years ago.

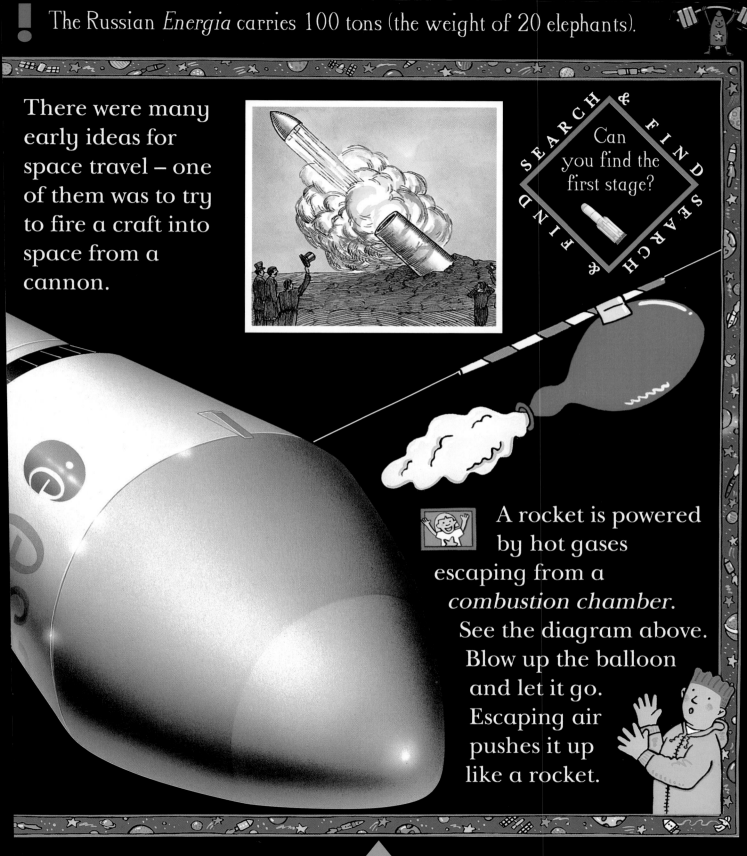

There were many early ideas for space travel – one of them was to try to fire a craft into space from a cannon.

SEARCH & FIND
Can you find the first stage?
FIND SEARCH & FIND SEARCH &

A rocket is powered by hot gases escaping from a *combustion chamber*. See the diagram above. Blow up the balloon and let it go. Escaping air pushes it up like a rocket.

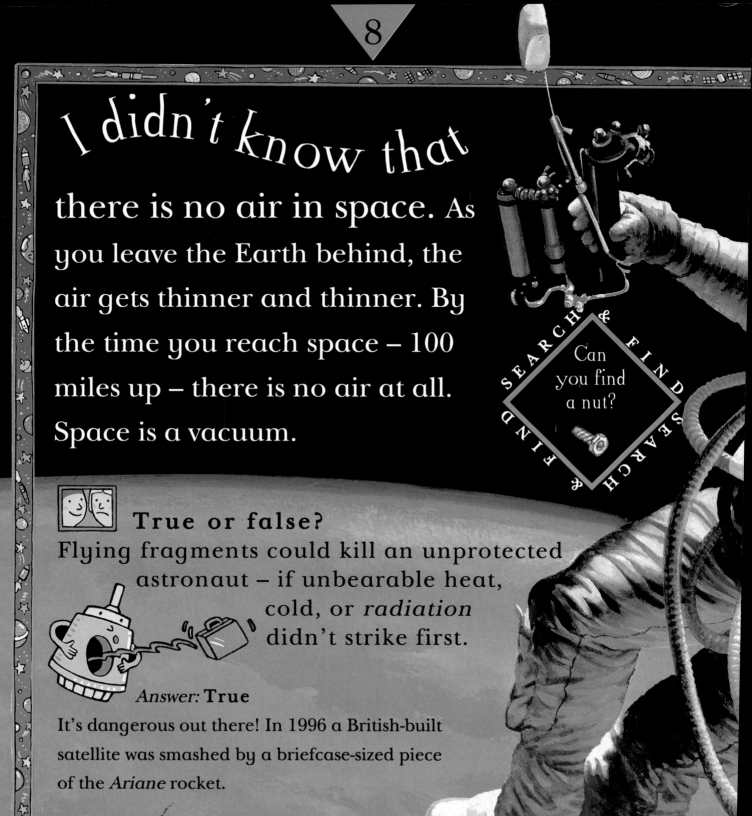

I didn't know that

there is no air in space. As you leave the Earth behind, the air gets thinner and thinner. By the time you reach space – 100 miles up – there is no air at all. Space is a vacuum.

SEARCH & FIND • FIND & SEARCH

Can you find a nut?

True or false?
Flying fragments could kill an unprotected astronaut – if unbearable heat, cold, or *radiation* didn't strike first.

Answer: **True**
It's dangerous out there! In 1996 a British-built satellite was smashed by a briefcase-sized piece of the *Ariane* rocket.

Astronauts need headsets in their helmets to communicate.

!
WARNING
ADULT
HELP NEEDED

Nothing burns without oxygen. Watch a candle go out when it has used all the oxygen in the jar. Water fills the space left by the oxygen. Because space has no air, spacecraft carry liquid oxygen to burn fuel.

Use coins to hold up jar.

The cosmonaut Alexei Leonov made the first-ever space walk way back in March 1965. He floated in space for 20 minutes before struggling back into the tiny spacecraft, *Voshkod 2.*

9

I didn't know that

you can jump higher on the Moon. Astronauts on the Moon can run and leap much farther than on the Earth. This is because the Moon's gravity is a lot weaker.

Your weight on the Moon is one sixth of your Earth weight. Can you figure out how much you would weigh if you were standing on the Moon?

The Moon has wide plains, which are called seas, but there is no water!

Jules Verne wrote a book called *From the Earth to the Moon* in 1865. He didn't realize that there was no air on the Moon!

SEARCH & FIND
FIND & SEARCH
Can you find the spaceship?

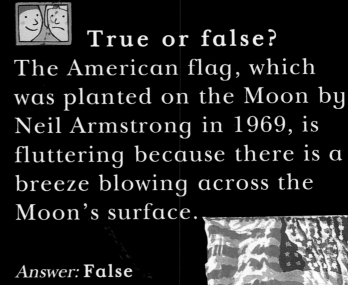

True or false?
The American flag, which was planted on the Moon by Neil Armstrong in 1969, is fluttering because there is a breeze blowing across the Moon's surface.

Answer: **False**
There is no air or wind on the Moon. The flag is held up by a metal rod.

Because there is no gravity in space, astronauts have to be strapped down for sleeping or going to the bathroom. Water would fly all over the place, so the toilet removes waste by suction....

I didn't know that

there are people living in space. Since 1971 people have been living for short periods on board space stations. These are in orbit 250 miles above the Earth. The Russian space station *Mir*, meaning "peace," has been in orbit since 1986.

Spiders, fish, monkeys, and dogs have all tried floating in space.

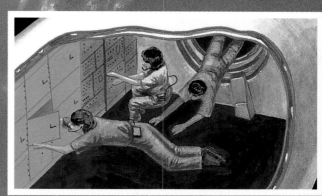

Astronauts need strict routines for working and resting to make life in space seem more normal. They exercise for at least two hours a day to keep their muscles strong.

 True or false? American astronauts have boarded the Russian space station *Mir*.

Answer: **True**
The space station has docking ports, which other spacecraft use. The Space Shuttle docked with *Mir* several times. An American woman spent a record six months on board.

SEARCH & FIND
Can you find a *Soyuz* spacecraft?
SEARCH & FIND

We call spacemen astronauts, which means "sailors of the stars." Russian spacemen are called cosmonauts, which means "sailors of the universe."

The first person to go into space was a Russian test pilot, Yuri Gagarin. In April 1961, his tiny spacecraft orbited the Earth once before reentering the *atmosphere.*

I didn't know that

astronauts are water-cooled.

Their underwear is threaded with liquid-filled tubes to keep their bodies at a steady temperature. Otherwise they might boil or freeze outside the spacecraft.

SEARCH & FIND
Can you find the second astronaut?
FIND & SEARCH

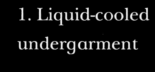

1. Liquid-cooled undergarment

2. Multilayered space suit

An astronaut can spend several hours outside the spacecraft in an MMU (Manned Maneuvering Unit). The space suit and the MMU form a life-support system with oxygen and cooling fluids, a snack to eat, and even a diaper!

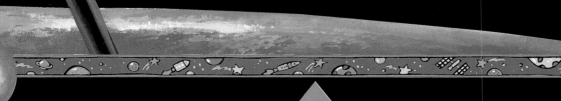

After reentry, landing a spacecraft safely is the hardest part of the journey. The first space travelers had to abandon their craft four miles above the Earth and parachute to safety.

I didn't know that

the Space Shuttle is covered in tiles. Heatproof tiles prevent a spacecraft from burning up when it reenters the Earth's atmosphere. Then it can be used again.

SEARCH & FIND & SEARCH & FIND
Can you find the green tile?

There have been around 80 successful Shuttle trips into space.

The Space Shuttle can be flown to its launch site on a jumbo jet's back.

 True or false?
The Space Shuttle is completely reusable.

Answer: **False**

1. The Shuttle's main fuel tank falls away and is not reused. 2. Parts of the rocket boosters are reused.

3. The orbiter glides to a safe landing and can be used again.

3

1

2

Three astronauts escaped from an explosion on board *Apollo 13*. Seven others were killed in 1986 when the Space Shuttle blew up.

I didn't know that

there's a telescope in space.

A space telescope can view space without Earth's atmosphere getting in the way. The Hubble Space Telescope was put into orbit 384 miles above the Earth in 1990.

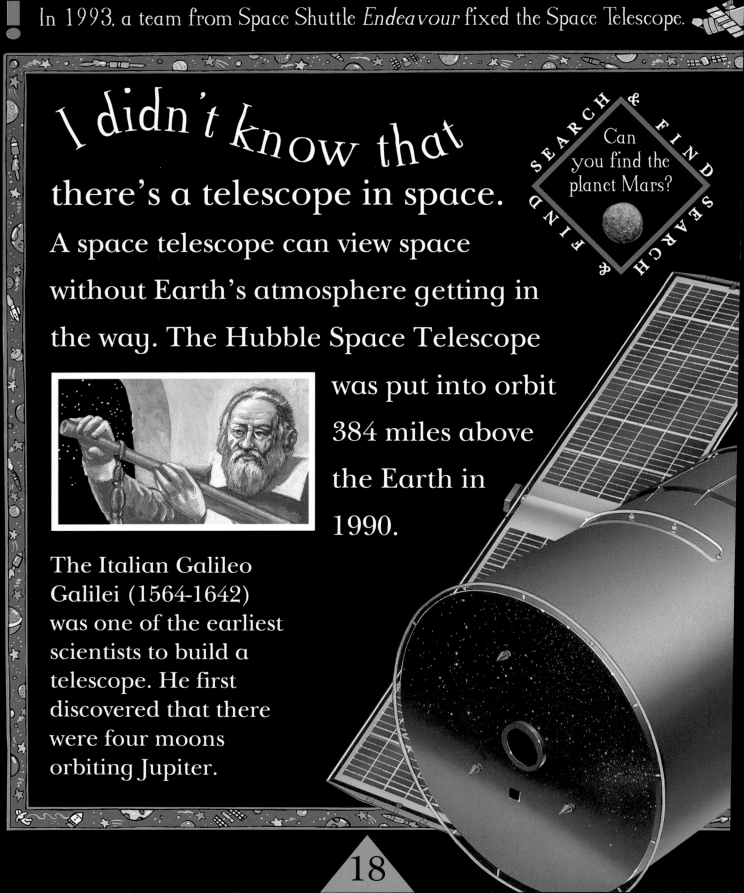

Can you find the planet Mars?

The Italian Galileo Galilei (1564-1642) was one of the earliest scientists to build a telescope. He first discovered that there were four moons orbiting Jupiter.

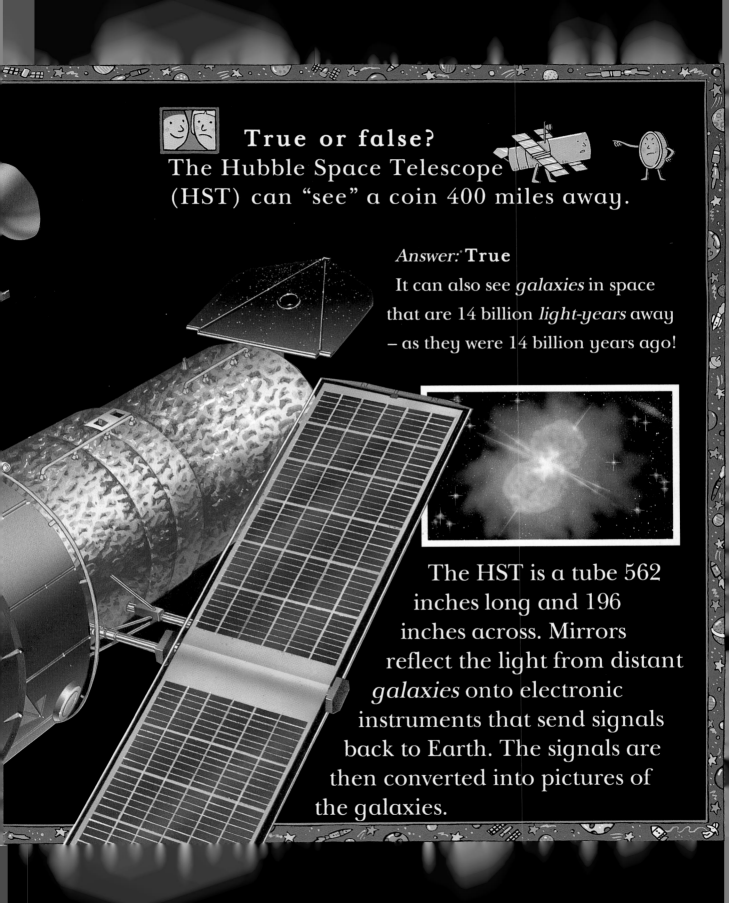

True or false?
The Hubble Space Telescope
(HST) can "see" a coin 400 miles away.

Answer: **True**
It can also see *galaxies* in space
that are 14 billion *light-years* away
– as they were 14 billion years ago!

The HST is a tube 562
inches long and 196
inches across. Mirrors
reflect the light from distant
galaxies onto electronic
instruments that send signals
back to Earth. The signals are
then converted into pictures of
the galaxies.

Sputnik 2 carried a dog called Laika ("traveling companion").

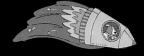

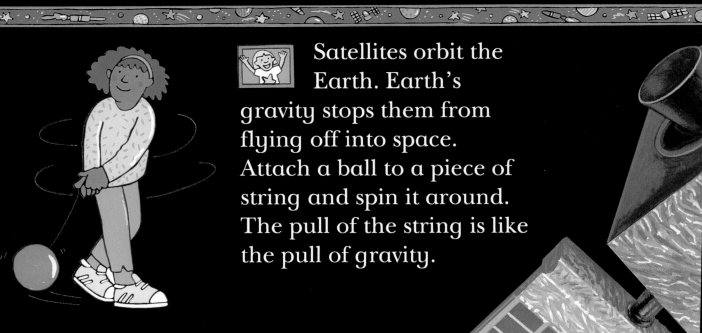

Satellites orbit the Earth. Earth's gravity stops them from flying off into space. Attach a ball to a piece of string and spin it around. The pull of the string is like the pull of gravity.

True or false?
Satellites eventually fall back to Earth.

Answer: **False**
Only those satellites in low orbits fall back to Earth and burn up. Those farther out in space will remain in orbit for millions of years.

SEARCH & FIND
Can you find the Space Shuttle?
FIND & SEARCH

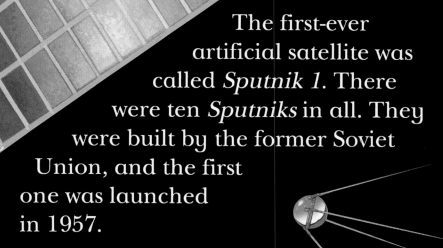

The first-ever artificial satellite was called *Sputnik 1*. There were ten *Sputniks* in all. They were built by the former Soviet Union, and the first one was launched in 1957.

I didn't know that satellites are powered by the Sun. As they travel around the Earth, satellites need electricity to power them. This is supplied by solar cells. Large arrays of solar panels convert the energy from the sun into electricity to replenish the satellites' batteries.

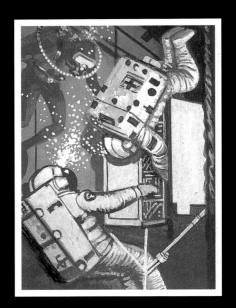

Members of the repair team have to be able to work in zero gravity while wearing space suits. Some of their training takes place in a water tank so they can get used to floating about.

SEARCH & FIND
Can you find another satellite?
FIND & SEARCH

I didn't know that

astronauts fix broken satellites in space. Space engineers are specially trained to recover faulty satellites and repair them. They work from the cargo bay of the Space Shuttle.

True or false?
Space Shuttles have arms and hands.

Answer: **True**
The jointed robot arm on a Space Shuttle has a hand on the end that can grip objects in space. It is operated from inside the Shuttle.

An astronaut with an MMU becomes a human satellite. The word *satellite* describes one thing that is in orbit around another. For example, the Moon is a satellite of the Earth.

I didn't know that

a *Viking* has landed on Mars.

Two *Viking* probes went to Mars in 1976. The landers were like mini-laboratories that took photos and analyzed samples. They sent information to Earth for six years.

SEARCH & FIND
Can you find a *Viking* mother ship?

True or false?
There are signs of life on Mars.

Answer: **True**
Tiny volcanic *organisms* have been found in a *meteorite* that came from Mars. The meteorite was discovered on Earth in the polar ice at the South Pole.

Early *astronomers* studying Mars noticed lines crisscrossing its surface. They thought the lines must be canals built by intelligent martians!

The *Viking* lander starts out inside the cone-shaped bioshield. 1. It separates from the mother ship above Mars. 2. It fires rockets to enter Mars' atmosphere. 3. It jettisons (dumps) the bioshield. The legs are lowered and the lander parachutes down. 4. Little *retro-rockets* provide a gentle landing.

1

2

3

4

Mars really is red, from the iron oxide (rust) in the soil.

Voyager's pictures showed that Jupiter's Red Spot is a giant storm.

I didn't know that

a robot is lost in space. The *Voyager* space probes launched in 1977 visited Jupiter, Saturn, Uranus, and Neptune. Although lost far out in the *Solar System* they act like robots and still send signals to Earth.

SEARCH & FIND & SEARCH & FIND
Can you find 18 moons?

Venera

True or false? Probes have only landed on Mars.

Answer: **False**
Probes have landed on Venus and relayed information to Earth before being crushed by the Venusian atmosphere.

Pictures sent back from Halley's Comet by the space probe *Giotto* showed that the nucleus (or center) is a city-sized lump of ice and dust.

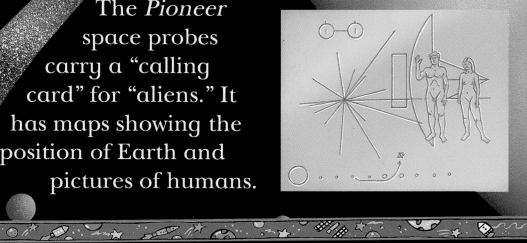

Voyager

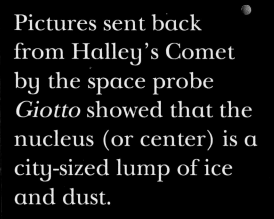

Giotto

The *Pioneer* space probes carry a "calling card" for "aliens." It has maps showing the position of Earth and pictures of humans.

The *Voyager* spacecraft operate on *nuclear power.*

I didn't know that

one day people will land on Mars. People could live on Mars in the future, but they would have to stay under cover. There are plans for six astronauts to spend 30 days there.

SEARCH & FIND
Can you find a *Viking* lander?
FIND SEARCH & FIND

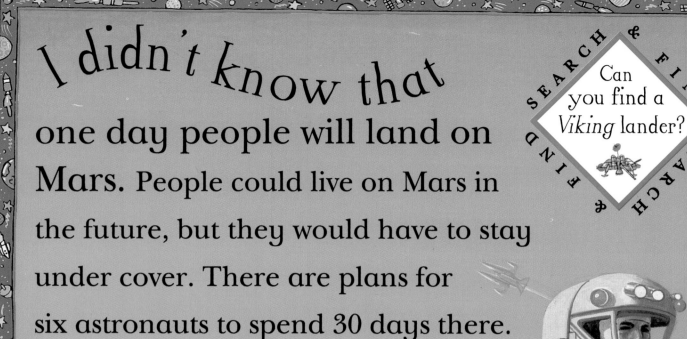

The famous film *2001: A Space Odyssey* is based on a story by the writer Arthur C. Clarke, and mentions Jupiter's moon, Europa.

Many more people might get their first taste of living in space on the International Space Station, a scientific institute that will soon be built in space. Lots of different countries are funding it.

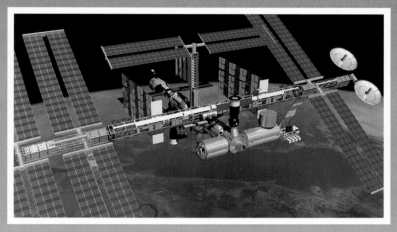

Space travel has come a long way. Less than a hundred years ago intelligent people thought a journey to the Moon was a crazy idea!

The journey alone to Mars would take nearly two years.

Glossary

Astronomer
Someone who studies the stars and the planets.

Atmosphere (Earth's)
The protective layer of gases around the planet.

Combustion chamber
The part of a rocket where the fuel and oxidizer combine and burn.

Galaxy
A collection of millions of stars.

Gravity
The natural "pull" of one object on another. Earth's gravity keeps us on the ground.

Light-year
5,880,000 million miles – the distance traveled by a ray of light in one year.

Meteorite
A piece of rock or metal from space that lands on Earth.

Nuclear power
Space probes on long journeys carry nuclear powerpacks that convert the energy of radioactive plutonium into electrical power.

Orbit
The path around a star or a planet taken by an object moving through space.

Organism
Any life-form, including those with very few cells such as bacteria and viruses.

Radiation
Harmful radiation contains particles and gamma rays emitted after a nuclear reaction.

Retro-rockets
Rockets that drive a spacecraft backward, to slow it down.

Satellite
Artificial satellites orbiting in space are used for communications, navigation, weather reports, and spying.

Solar System
Our Sun and everything that orbits around it.

Space probe
A fully-automated spacecraft that sends back information.

Index